MASTERING IT SALES: PROVEN STRATEGIES FOR SUCCESS IN THE TECH INDUSTRY

By: Mike Angerami

ABSTRACT

In the rapidly evolving world of Information Technology (IT), generating sales is both a science and an art. This comprehensive book, Generating Sales in IT: Strategies, Techniques, and Best Practices, serves as an essential guide for sales professionals navigating the unique challenges and opportunities within the IT sector. Spanning 34 detailed chapters, the book covers every facet of IT sales, from understanding the industry's landscape and building effective sales strategies to leveraging advanced technologies and overcoming common sales obstacles. Readers will gain insights into the modern IT sales process, the role of technology, and the importance of understanding the IT buyer's decision-making process. The book delves into the nuances of setting realistic sales goals, developing winning sales plans, and utilizing both inbound and outbound lead generation strategies. It also explores advanced techniques such as solution selling, consultative selling, and value-based selling, all tailored to the IT Industry. The book further addresses critical aspects such as post-sales engagement, customer success, and measuring sales performance through key metrics. It highlights the impact of digital transformation, the integration of AI and automation in sales, and the importance of data-driven strategies. With practical advice on managing sales teams, conducting international sales, and adhering to legal and ethical standards, this book equips readers with the knowledge to excel in IT Sales. Real-world case studies, expert interviews, and examples of successful sales campaigns provide actionable insights and inspiration. Appendices offer additional resources, including templates, glossaries, and directories of useful tools and associations. Whether you are a seasoned sales professional or new to the IT industry, Generating Sales in IT is a vital resource that will help you navigate the complexities of IT sales and achieve sustained success in a competitive market. the rapidly evolving world of Information Technology (IT), generating sales is both a science and an art. This comprehensive book, Generating Sales in IT: Strategies, Techniques, and Best Practices, serves as an essential guide for sales professionals navigating the unique challenges and opportunities within the IT sector. Spanning 34 detailed chapters, the book covers every facet of IT sales, from understanding the

TABLE OF CONTENTS

Chapter 1: Overview of the IT Industry..........................1

Chapter 2: The IT Sales Process...............................5

Chapter 3: The Role of Technology in IT Sales................9

Chapter 4: Understanding the IT Buyer.......................13

Chapter 5: Market Research and Analysis....................17

Chapter 6: Setting Sales Goals and Objectives..............21

Chapter 7: Developing a Sales Plan...............................25

Chapter 8: Lead Generation Strategies........................29

Chapter 9: Prospecting Techniques.............................33

Chapter 10: Sales Pitch Development..........................37

Chapter 11: Building Relationships with Clients............41

Chapter 12: Negotiation and Closing Techniques..........45

Chapter 13: Post-Sales Engagement...........................49

Chapter 14: Measuring Sales Performance..................53

Chapter 15: Advanced Sales Techniques.....................57

Chapter 16: Sales Enablement………………………..61

Chapter 17: Digital Transformation in Sales……………..65

Chapter 18: Using AI and Automation in Sales……………69

Chapter 19: Data-Driven Sales Strategies………………73

Chapter 20: Personalization in Sales…………………..77

Chapter 21: Account-Based Marketing………………….81

Chapter 22: Managing Sales Teams…………………….85

Chapter 23: International Sales………………………89

Chapter 24: Legal and Ethical Considerations in Sales….93

Chapter 25: Successful IT Sales Campaigns………………97

Chapter 26: Overcoming Sales Challenges……………….101

Chapter 27: Innovation in IT Sales……………………105

Chapter 28: Sales Failures and What We Can Learn……109

Chapter 29: Customer Testimonials and Feedback………113

Chapter 30: Interviews with Industry Experts……………117

Chapter 31: Regional and Sector-Specific Strategies…..121

Chapter 32: Emerging Markets and Opportunities……….125

Chapter 33: The Future of IT Sales……………………129

Chapter 34: Summary and Key Takeaways.....................133

Appendix A: Glossary of IT Sales Terms........................137

Appendix B: Templates and Worksheets.......................139

Appendix C: Recommended Reading and Resources.......141

Appendix D: Sales Tools and Software Directory.............143

Appendix E: Industry Associations and Networks............145

Appendix F: Frequently Asked Questions........................147

CHAPTER 1: OVERVIEW OF THE IT INDUSTRY

HISTORY AND EVOLUTION

The Information Technology (IT) industry has experienced rapid growth and transformation since its inception. The industry began in the mid-20th century with the development of the first computers. Early computers were large, expensive, and limited to government and research institutions. However, the invention of the microprocessor in the 1970s revolutionized the industry, making computers more accessible and affordable for businesses and eventually consumers.

The 1980s and 1990s saw the rise of personal computers, networking technologies, and the internet. Companies like IBM, Microsoft, and Apple became household names. The internet boom of the late 1990s and early 2000s further accelerated the industry's growth, leading to the development of new technologies and business models.

Today, the IT industry encompasses a wide range of technologies, including cloud computing, artificial intelligence (AI), big data, cybersecurity, and the Internet of Things (IoT). The industry continues to evolve at a rapid pace, driven by innovation and the increasing integration of technology into all aspects of society.

KEY SEGMENTS AND MARKETS

The IT industry is diverse, with numerous segments and markets. Some of the key segments include:

- Hardware: This segment includes the production and sale of physical devices such as computers, servers, networking equipment, and peripherals.
- Software: Software development is a major segment, encompassing operating systems, applications, and software services.
- Services: IT services include consulting, system integration, managed services, and support.
- Telecommunications: This segment involves the transmission of data and includes internet service providers, mobile operators, and networking solutions.
- Cloud Computing: Cloud services, including Infrastructure as a Service (IaaS), Platform as a Service (PaaS), and Software as a Service (SaaS), are a rapidly growing segment.
- Cybersecurity: This segment focuses on protecting systems and data from cyber threats.
- Artificial Intelligence and Machine Learning: AI and ML are transforming industries by enabling automation, predictive analytics, and advanced decision-making.

CURRENT TRENDS AND FUTURE DIRECTIONS

The IT industry is characterized by constant innovation and change. Some of the current trends shaping the industry include:

- Digital Transformation: Organizations are leveraging technology to improve operations, enhance customer experiences, and create new business models.
- Cloud Adoption: The shift to cloud computing continues to accelerate, driven by the need for scalability, flexibility, and cost efficiency.
- AI and Automation: AI and automation are being integrated into various processes, from customer service to manufacturing, driving efficiency and innovation.
- Cybersecurity: With the increase in cyber threats, cybersecurity has become a top priority for businesses and governments.
- IoT: The Internet of Things is expanding, with more connected devices and systems, leading to new applications and opportunities.
- Data Analytics: The ability to collect, analyze, and derive insights from large datasets is becoming critical for decision-making and strategy.
- Remote Work: The COVID-19 pandemic has accelerated the adoption of remote work technologies, changing the way businesses operate.

The future of the IT industry will likely be shaped by advancements in quantum computing, 5G networks, and the continued integration of AI and machine learning into everyday applications. As technology continues to evolve, businesses will need to stay agile and adapt to new trends and challenges.

CHAPTER 2: THE IT SALES PROCESS

Traditional vs. Modern Sales Processes

The sales process in the IT industry has evolved significantly over the years. Traditional sales processes often involved a linear approach, starting with lead generation, followed by prospecting, pitching, handling objections, and closing the sale. This approach was largely transactional and focused on short-term gains.

Modern sales processes, however, are more dynamic and customer-centric. They involve understanding the customer's needs and providing tailored solutions. This approach emphasizes building long-term relationships and ensuring customer satisfaction. Key aspects of modern sales processes include:

- Consultative Selling: Engaging with clients to understand their problems and offering customized solutions.
- Solution Selling: Focusing on the overall solution rather than individual products or services.
- Inbound Sales: Attracting customers through valuable content and engaging with them on their terms.

SALES CYCLE IN IT

The sales cycle in the IT industry typically involves several stages:

1. Lead Generation: Identifying potential customers through various channels such as online marketing, social media, referrals, and networking.
2. Qualification: Assessing the leads to determine if they meet the criteria for a potential sale.
3. Needs Analysis: Understanding the specific needs and challenges of the prospective customer.
4. Proposal: Crafting a tailored solution and presenting a proposal to the client.
5. Negotiation: Discussing terms, addressing objections, and negotiating the deal.
6. Closing: Finalizing the agreement and securing the sale.
7. Implementation: Delivering the product or service and ensuring it meets the customer's expectations.
8. Follow-Up: Maintaining contact with the customer to ensure satisfaction and identify opportunities for upselling or cross-selling.

UNIQUE CHALLENGES IN IT SALES

Selling IT products and services presents unique challenges compared to other industries. These include:

- Complexity of Products: IT solutions are often complex and require a deep understanding of the technology.
- Rapid Technological Changes: The fast pace of technological advancements means that sales teams must continuously update their knowledge.
- Long Sales Cycles: Due to the complexity and high costs involved, IT sales cycles can be lengthy and require persistent effort.
- Multiple Decision-Makers: IT purchases often involve multiple stakeholders, each with their own priorities and concerns.

CHAPTER 3: THE ROLE OF TECHNOLOGY IN IT SALES

CRM SYSTEMS AND SALES AUTOMATION

Customer Relationship Management (CRM) systems are crucial tools in modern IT sales. They help sales teams manage customer interactions, track sales activities, and streamline processes. Key benefits of CRM systems include:

- Centralized Data: Storing all customer information in one place for easy access and management.
- Automation: Automating repetitive tasks such as follow-up emails and data entry, allowing sales teams to focus on high-value activities.
- Analytics: Providing insights into sales performance, customer behavior, and trends to inform strategy.

AI AND MACHINE LEARNING IN SALES

Artificial Intelligence (AI) and Machine Learning (ML) are transforming IT sales by enabling more precise targeting, personalization, and efficiency. Applications of AI and ML in sales include:

- Predictive Analytics: Analyzing data to predict customer behavior and identify the most promising leads.
- Personalized Recommendations: Using algorithms to suggest products or services that best match the customer's needs.
- Chatbots and Virtual Assistants: Providing instant support and engagement through automated chat systems.

DATA ANALYTICS AND SALES FORECASTING

Data analytics is critical for making informed sales decisions. By analyzing historical data, sales teams can identify patterns and trends that guide strategy. Key aspects of data analytics in sales include:

- Sales Forecasting: Predicting future sales based on historical data, market trends, and other factors.
- Performance Analysis: Assessing the effectiveness of sales strategies and identifying areas for improvement.
- Customer Insights: Understanding customer preferences and behaviors to tailor sales approaches.

CHAPTER 4: UNDERSTANDING THE IT BUYER

IT BUYER PERSONAS

Understanding the various personas involved in IT purchasing decisions is crucial for tailoring sales strategies. Key personas include:

- The Technical Buyer: Often a CTO or IT manager, this persona focuses on the technical aspects and feasibility of the solution.
- The Economic Buyer: Typically a CFO or procurement officer, this persona is concerned with the financial impact and ROI.
- The User Buyer: These are the end-users who will interact with the solution daily. Their input is critical for ensuring the solution meets practical needs.
- The Influencer: An internal or external consultant who influences the decision-making process with their expertise and opinions.

DECISION-MAKING PROCESS

The IT buying decision is usually a collective process involving multiple stakeholders. The steps typically include:

1. Problem Identification: Recognizing a need or problem that requires a solution.
2. Research and Exploration: Gathering information about potential solutions and vendors.
3. Evaluation: Comparing different options based on features, pricing, and vendor reputation.
4. Decision: Selecting the solution that best meets the organization's needs.
5. Approval: Obtaining the necessary approvals from senior management or procurement.
6. Purchase: Finalizing the purchase agreement and implementation plan.

PAIN POINTS AND NEEDS ANALYSIS

Identifying and addressing the specific pain points of IT buyers is essential for effective selling. Common pain points include:

- Scalability: The need for solutions that can grow with the business.
- Security: Ensuring the solution protects against cyber threats.
- Integration: Compatibility with existing systems and infrastructure.
- Cost: Balancing budget constraints with the need for high-quality solutions.
- Support and Maintenance: Availability of reliable customer support and ongoing maintenance.

CHAPTER 5: MARKET RESEARCH AND ANALYSIS

CONDUCTING MARKET RESEARCH

Thorough market research is the foundation of successful IT sales strategies. Steps for conducting effective market research include:

- Define Objectives: Clearly outline what you want to learn from the research.
- Identify Target Market: Determine the specific segments you want to analyze.
- Collect Data: Use a mix of primary (surveys, interviews) and secondary (industry reports, competitor analysis) data sources.
- Analyze Data: Look for patterns, trends, and insights that can inform your sales strategies.

ANALYZING COMPETITORS

Competitive analysis helps you understand your position in the market and identify opportunities for differentiation. Key elements include:

- Competitor Identification: List your main competitors in the market.
- Strengths and Weaknesses: Analyze their strengths and weaknesses compared to your offerings.
- Market Positioning: Understand how competitors position themselves in the market.
- Strategies and Tactics: Identify the strategies and tactics they use to attract customers.

IDENTIFYING OPPORTUNITIES AND THREATS

A SWOT analysis (Strengths, Weaknesses, Opportunities, Threats) helps in identifying internal and external factors that can impact your sales efforts. Key considerations include:

- Opportunities: New markets, emerging trends, and technological advancements.
- Threats: Competitive pressures, market saturation, and economic fluctuations.

CHAPTER 6: SETTING SALES GOALS AND OBJECTIVES

SMART GOALS

Setting clear, achievable sales goals is critical for guiding your team's efforts. The SMART criteria help ensure your goals are:

- Specific: Clearly define what you want to achieve.
- Measurable: Establish criteria to track progress.
- Achievable: Set realistic goals that are attainable.
- Relevant: Ensure the goals align with overall business objectives.
- Time-bound: Set a deadline for achieving the goals.

KEY PERFORMANCE INDICATORS (KPIS)

KPIs are metrics used to evaluate the success of your sales efforts. Common KPIs in IT sales include:

- Sales Revenue: Total revenue generated from sales.
- Lead Conversion Rate: Percentage of leads that convert into customers.
- Customer Acquisition Cost (CAC): Cost of acquiring a new customer.
- Customer Lifetime Value (CLV): Total revenue expected from a customer over their lifetime.
- Sales Cycle Length: Time taken to convert a lead into a customer.

ALIGNING SALES GOALS WITH BUSINESS OBJECTIVES

Ensure that your sales goals are aligned with the broader business objectives. This alignment helps in:

- Strategic Coherence: Ensuring all efforts contribute to the overall mission.
- Resource Allocation: Efficiently allocating resources to achieve strategic goals.
- Performance Measurement: Evaluating performance based on strategic priorities.

CHAPTER 7: DEVELOPING A SALES PLAN

COMPONENTS OF A SALES PLAN

A well-structured sales plan is essential for guiding your sales team's efforts and achieving your sales goals. Key components of a sales plan include:

- Executive Summary: An overview of the sales plan, including objectives and key strategies.
- Market Analysis: A detailed analysis of the market, including target segments and competitive landscape.
- Sales Objectives: Clear, measurable goals that align with overall business objectives.
- Sales Strategies: Specific strategies and tactics for achieving sales objectives.
- Action Plan: A step-by-step plan for implementing sales strategies, including timelines and responsibilities.
- Budget: A detailed budget outlining the financial resources required to execute the sales plan.
- Performance Metrics: KPIs and other metrics for measuring the success of the sales plan.

SALES PLANNING TECHNIQUES

Effective sales planning involves several techniques, including:

- SWOT Analysis: Identifying strengths, weaknesses, opportunities, and threats to inform your sales strategy.
- Customer Segmentation: Dividing the market into segments based on characteristics such as industry, size, and needs.
- Sales Funnel Management: Tracking and managing prospects through the stages of the sales funnel to improve conversion rates.
- Forecasting: Using historical data and market trends to predict future sales and set realistic targets.

IMPLEMENTING THE SALES PLAN

Successful implementation of a sales plan requires:

- Clear Communication: Ensuring that all team members understand the plan and their roles in executing it.
- Training and Support: Providing the necessary training and resources to enable your team to execute the plan effectively.
- Monitoring and Adjustment: Continuously monitoring progress and making adjustments as needed to stay on track.

CHAPTER 8: LEAD GENERATION STRATEGIES

Inbound vs. Outbound Lead Generation

Lead generation can be categorized into inbound and outbound strategies:

- Inbound Lead Generation: Attracting potential customers through content marketing, SEO, social media, and other methods that draw prospects to your business.
- Outbound Lead Generation: Actively reaching out to potential customers through methods such as cold calling, email marketing, and direct mail.

CONTENT MARKETING FOR LEAD GENERATION

Content marketing is a powerful inbound lead generation strategy. Key tactics include:

- Blogging: Creating valuable, informative blog posts that address the needs and interests of your target audience.
- E-books and Whitepapers: Offering in-depth resources that provide valuable insights and solutions to your audience's problems.
- Webinars: Hosting online seminars that educate and engage your audience while showcasing your expertise.

SOCIAL MEDIA AND SEO

Leveraging social media and SEO can significantly boost your lead generation efforts:

- Social Media: Using platforms like LinkedIn, Twitter, and Facebook to connect with potential customers and share valuable content.
- SEO: Optimizing your website and content to rank higher in search engine results, making it easier for prospects to find you.

CHAPTER 9: PROSPECTING TECHNIQUES

IDENTIFYING POTENTIAL CLIENTS

Effective prospecting starts with identifying potential clients who are a good fit for your products or services. Techniques include:

- Target Market Definition: Clearly defining your target market based on factors such as industry, company size, and location.
- Buyer Personas: Creating detailed profiles of your ideal customers to guide your prospecting efforts.
- Lead Lists: Using databases and lead generation tools to compile lists of potential clients.

EFFECTIVE PROSPECTING METHODS

Prospecting methods vary, but some of the most effective include:

- Cold Calling: Reaching out to potential clients by phone to introduce your products or services.
- Email Campaigns: Sending targeted email campaigns to prospects with personalized messages.
- Networking: Attending industry events, conferences, and meetups to connect with potential clients in person.

LEVERAGING NETWORKING AND REFERRALS

Building a strong network and leveraging referrals can greatly enhance your prospecting efforts:

- Networking: Establishing relationships with industry contacts who can refer potential clients to you.
- Referral Programs: Creating programs that incentivize existing clients and partners to refer new business.

CHAPTER 10: SALES PITCH DEVELOPMENT

CRAFTING A COMPELLING VALUE PROPOSITION

A compelling value proposition clearly communicates the benefits of your product or service and why it's the best choice for the customer. Key elements include:

- Clarity: Clearly state what your product or service does.
- Benefits: Highlight the specific benefits and value it provides.
- Differentiation: Explain how your offering is unique compared to competitors.

TAILORING THE PITCH TO DIFFERENT AUDIENCES

Tailoring your sales pitch to different audiences increases its effectiveness. Considerations include:

- Understanding the Audience: Knowing the specific needs, pain points, and priorities of the audience.
- Customizing the Message: Adjusting your message to address the unique concerns of each audience segment.
- Using Relevant Examples: Providing examples and case studies that resonate with the audience.

PRESENTATION SKILLS AND TECHNIQUES

Effective presentation skills are crucial for delivering a successful sales pitch. Tips include:

- Practice: Rehearse your pitch multiple times to ensure a smooth delivery.
- Engagement: Engage the audience with eye contact, questions, and interactive elements.
- Visual Aids: Use visual aids such as slides, demos, and videos to enhance your presentation.

CHAPTER 11: BUILDING RELATIONSHIPS WITH CLIENTS

IMPORTANCE OF RELATIONSHIP BUILDING

Building strong relationships with clients is essential for long-term success. Benefits include:

- Trust and Loyalty: Building trust leads to client loyalty and repeat business.
- Referrals: Satisfied clients are more likely to refer new business.
- Customer Retention: Strong relationships improve customer retention rates.

TECHNIQUES FOR BUILDING TRUST

Building trust with clients involves:

- Transparency: Being open and honest in all interactions.
- Reliability: Consistently delivering on promises and commitments.
- Communication: Maintaining regular, clear communication with clients.

LONG-TERM CLIENT RELATIONSHIP MANAGEMENT

Managing client relationships over the long term requires:

- Regular Check-Ins: Scheduling regular check-ins to discuss progress and address any concerns.
- Personalization: Personalizing interactions and solutions to meet the unique needs of each client.
- Proactive Support: Providing proactive support and anticipating client needs before they arise.

Effective e-commerce and online sales strategies include:

- User-Friendly Website: Ensure your website is easy to navigate and provides a seamless user experience.
- SEO: Optimize your website and content for search engines to attract organic traffic.
- Digital Advertising: Use digital advertising to target potential customers and drive traffic to your website.

CHAPTER 18: USING AI AND AUTOMATION IN SALES

AI-POWERED SALES TOOLS

AI-powered tools can enhance your sales efforts. Key applications include:

- Lead Scoring: Using AI to score and prioritize leads based on their likelihood to convert.
- Sales Forecasting: Leveraging AI to predict future sales and trends.
- Chatbots: Implementing chatbots to engage with website visitors and answer common questions.

CHATBOTS AND VIRTUAL ASSISTANTS

Chatbots and virtual assistants can improve customer engagement and support. Benefits include:

- 24/7 Availability: Providing support and information to customers at any time.
- Instant Responses: Offering quick responses to common questions and issues.
- Lead Generation: Engaging with website visitors to capture leads and contact information.

AUTOMATING SALES PROCESSES

Automating sales processes can improve efficiency and consistency. Key areas for automation include:

- Email Campaigns: Automating email campaigns to nurture leads and keep them engaged.
- Follow-Up: Setting up automated follow-up sequences to ensure timely communication with leads.
- Data Entry: Automating data entry tasks to reduce administrative burden and minimize errors.

CHAPTER 19: DATA-DRIVEN SALES STRATEGIES

IMPORTANCE OF DATA IN SALES

Data is a critical asset for informed decision-making in sales. Benefits of data-driven sales strategies include:

- Improved Targeting: Using data to identify and prioritize high-potential leads.
- Personalization: Tailoring sales messages and offers based on customer data and insights.
- Performance Measurement: Tracking and analyzing sales performance to identify areas for improvement.

ANALYZING SALES DATA

Key steps for analyzing sales data include:

- Data Collection: Collect data from various sources, including CRM systems, sales reports, and customer interactions.
- Data Cleaning: Ensure data accuracy and consistency by cleaning and organizing the data.
- Data Analysis: Use analytical tools and techniques to interpret data and gain insights.

CHAPTER 20: PERSONALIZATION IN SALES

CUSTOMIZED SALES APPROACHES

Personalization in sales involves tailoring your approach to meet the specific needs and preferences of each customer. Strategies include:

- Personalized Emails: Use customer data to send personalized email communications that address specific needs and interests.
- Tailored Presentations: Customize sales presentations to highlight how your solution addresses the unique challenges of each prospect.
- One-to-One Meetings: Schedule individual meetings to discuss personalized solutions and build stronger relationships.

PERSONALIZING COMMUNICATION

Effective communication personalization techniques include:

- Using Customer Names: Address customers by their names in all communications to create a more personal connection.
- Relevant Content: Share content that is relevant to the customer's industry, role, and specific challenges.
- Follow-Up: Send personalized follow-up messages based on previous interactions and expressed interests.

TAILORING SOLUTIONS TO CLIENT NEEDS

Tailoring your solutions to meet the specific needs of each client involves:

- Understanding Needs: Conduct thorough needs assessments to understand the client's specific challenges and requirements.
- Custom Solutions: Develop customized solutions that directly address the identified needs and provide maximum value.
- Continuous Feedback: Regularly seek feedback from clients to ensure the solutions continue to meet their evolving needs.

CHAPTER 21: ACCOUNT-BASED MARKETING

ABM STRATEGIES AND TACTICS

Account-Based Marketing (ABM) involves focusing your marketing and sales efforts on specific high-value accounts. Key strategies include:

- Target Account Selection: Identify and prioritize high-value accounts that are a good fit for your solutions.
- Personalized Campaigns: Develop personalized marketing campaigns tailored to the specific needs and pain points of each target account.
- Collaboration: Foster close collaboration between marketing and sales teams to align efforts and maximize impact.

INTEGRATING SALES AND MARKETING

Effective ABM requires seamless integration between sales and marketing. Techniques include:

- Shared Goals: Establish shared goals and KPIs that align with both sales and marketing objectives.
- Regular Communication: Hold regular meetings and check-ins to ensure alignment and collaboration.
- Unified Messaging: Ensure consistent messaging and branding across all marketing and sales materials.

MEASURING ABM SUCCESS

Measuring the success of your ABM efforts involves:

- Account Engagement: Track engagement metrics such as email open rates, website visits, and event attendance for target accounts.
- Pipeline Contribution: Measure the contribution of ABM efforts to the sales pipeline and revenue.
- Customer Feedback: Collect feedback from target accounts to assess the impact and effectiveness of your ABM strategies.

CHAPTER 22: MANAGING SALES TEAMS

BUILDING A HIGH-PERFORMING SALES TEAM

Building a high-performing sales team involves:

- Recruiting Top Talent: Identify and recruit individuals with the skills, experience, and drive needed to succeed in sales.
- Onboarding: Provide comprehensive onboarding to ensure new hires understand your products, processes, and expectations.
- Ongoing Training: Offer continuous training and development opportunities to help your team stay updated and improve their skills.

LEADERSHIP AND MOTIVATION

Effective leadership and motivation techniques include:

- Clear Vision: Communicate a clear vision and direction for the sales team.
- Incentives: Implement incentive programs that reward high performance and motivate team members.
- Support: Provide the necessary support and resources to help your team achieve their goals.

PERFORMANCE MANAGEMENT

Managing sales team performance involves:

- Setting Expectations: Clearly define performance expectations and goals.
- Regular Reviews: Conduct regular performance reviews to provide feedback and identify areas for improvement.
- Coaching: Offer coaching and mentoring to help team members develop their skills and achieve their potential.

CHAPTER 23: INTERNATIONAL SALES

CHALLENGES OF SELLING GLOBALLY

Selling IT products and services internationally presents unique challenges, including:

- Cultural Differences: Understanding and respecting cultural differences that may impact sales interactions.
- Regulatory Compliance: Navigating different regulations and compliance requirements in each market.
- Logistics: Managing the logistics of delivering products and services across borders.

ADAPTING TO DIFFERENT MARKETS

Successfully adapting to different markets involves:

- Market Research: Conduct thorough research to understand the local market conditions, customer needs, and competitive landscape.
- Localization: Tailor your marketing materials, sales approaches, and product offerings to fit the local market.
- Local Partnerships: Establish partnerships with local businesses to enhance your market presence and credibility.

CROSS-CULTURAL SALES TECHNIQUES

Effective cross-cultural sales techniques include:

- Cultural Sensitivity: Show respect and sensitivity to cultural norms and practices.
- Communication: Adapt your communication style to match the preferences of the local market.
- Relationship Building: Focus on building strong relationships and trust with local customers and partners.

CHAPTER 24: LEGAL AND ETHICAL CONSIDERATIONS IN SALES

COMPLIANCE AND REGULATIONS

Compliance with legal and regulatory requirements is critical in IT sales. Key areas include:

- Data Protection: Ensure compliance with data protection regulations such as GDPR and CCPA.
- Anti-Bribery: Adhere to anti-bribery and anti-corruption laws in all sales interactions.
- Export Controls: Comply with export control regulations when selling products and services internationally.

ETHICAL SALES PRACTICES

Maintaining high ethical standards in sales involves:

- Honesty: Be transparent and honest in all communications with customers.
- Integrity: Adhere to ethical principles and avoid deceptive or manipulative tactics.
- Accountability: Take responsibility for your actions and address any issues that arise promptly and professionally.

HANDLING CONFIDENTIAL INFORMATION

Proper handling of confidential information is essential to maintain trust and comply with legal requirements. Best practices include:

- Secure Storage: Store confidential information securely to prevent unauthorized access.
- Limited Access: Restrict access to confidential information to only those who need it.
- Confidentiality Agreements: Use confidentiality agreements to protect sensitive information shared with clients and partners.

CHAPTER 25: SUCCESSFUL IT SALES CAMPAIGNS

DETAILED CASE STUDIES

Studying successful IT sales campaigns provides valuable insights. Key elements of successful campaigns include:

- Clear Objectives: Define clear, measurable objectives for the campaign.
- Targeted Approach: Identify and target specific customer segments that are most likely to benefit from your solution.
- Multi-Channel Strategy: Use a mix of marketing and sales channels to reach your target audience.
- Continuous Improvement: Monitor campaign performance and make adjustments to optimize results.

KEY SUCCESS FACTORS

Key factors contributing to the success of IT sales campaigns include:

- Customer Focus: Prioritize understanding and addressing the needs of the customer.
- Innovation: Use innovative approaches and technologies to stand out from competitors.
- Strong Team: Build a team with the skills, knowledge, and motivation to execute the campaign effectively.

LESSONS LEARNED

Analyzing the lessons learned from successful campaigns helps improve future efforts. Common lessons include:

- Flexibility: Be prepared to adapt your strategy based on feedback and changing conditions.
- Communication: Maintain clear and consistent communication with all stakeholders.
- Measurement: Track key metrics to measure success and identify areas for improvement.

Effective strategies for penetrating new markets include:

- Local Partnerships: Establish partnerships with local businesses to gain market insights and build credibility.
- Market Research: Conduct thorough market research to understand local needs, preferences, and competition.
- Adaptation: Adapt your products, services, and marketing strategies to fit the local market.

SUCCESS STORIES

Analyzing success stories provides valuable lessons for entering new markets. Key examples include:

- Technology Adoption: Study how companies have successfully introduced new technologies in emerging markets.
- Market Entry Strategies: Learn from the strategies used by successful companies to enter and grow in new markets.

CHAPTER 33: THE FUTURE OF IT SALES

PREDICTIONS FOR THE NEXT DECADE

Predictions for the future of IT sales include:

- Increased Automation: Greater use of AI and automation to streamline sales processes and improve efficiency.
- Personalization: Enhanced personalization of sales approaches and customer experiences.
- Data-Driven Decisions: Growing reliance on data analytics to inform sales strategies and decisions.

IMPACT OF EMERGING TECHNOLOGIES

Emerging technologies will have a significant impact on IT sales. Key technologies include:

- AI and Machine Learning: Advanced AI and machine learning algorithms will enable more accurate predictions and personalized experiences.
- Blockchain: Blockchain technology will enhance security and transparency in sales transactions.
- IoT: The Internet of Things will create new opportunities for connected products and services.

PREPARING FOR THE FUTURE

Preparing for the future of IT sales involves:

- Continuous Learning: Stay updated with the latest technological advancements and industry trends.
- Flexibility: Be adaptable and open to change in response to new developments.
- Strategic Planning: Develop long-term strategies that incorporate emerging technologies and trends.

CHAPTER 34: SUMMARY AND KEY TAKEAWAYS

RECAP OF MAJOR POINTS

The key points covered in this book include:

- Understanding the IT Sales Environment: The unique aspects and challenges of IT sales.
- Building a Winning Sales Strategy: Techniques for developing and implementing effective sales strategies.
- Advanced Sales Techniques and Technologies: Leveraging modern tools and techniques to enhance sales performance.
- Case Studies and Real-World Examples: Insights from successful and unsuccessful sales campaigns.
- Preparing for the Future: Adapting to emerging trends and technologies to stay competitive.

ACTIONABLE INSIGHTS

Key actionable insights for IT sales professionals include:

- Focus on the Customer: Prioritize understanding and meeting customer needs.
- Embrace Innovation: Continuously adopt new technologies and approaches to improve sales effectiveness.
- Build Strong Relationships: Foster long-term relationships with customers and partners.
- Measure and Improve: Regularly measure performance and make data-driven improvements.

FINAL THOUGHTS

The IT sales landscape is constantly evolving, presenting both challenges and opportunities. By staying informed, adaptable, and customer-focused, sales professionals can navigate this dynamic environment and achieve success.

APPENDICES AND ADDITIONAL RESOURCES

APPENDIX A: GLOSSARY OF IT SALES TERMS

- CRM: Customer Relationship Management
- AI: Artificial Intelligence
- ML: Machine Learning
- ROI: Return on Investment
- CLV: Customer Lifetime Value
- CAC: Customer Acquisition Cost
- ABM: Account-Based Marketing

APPENDIX B: TEMPLATES AND WORKSHEETS

- Sales Plan Template
- Lead Generation Worksheet
- Sales Pitch Development Template

APPENDIX C: RECOMMENDED READING AND RESOURCES

- "SPIN Selling" by Neil Rackham
- "The Challenger Sale" by Matthew Dixon and Brent Adamson
- "Predictable Revenue" by Aaron Ross and Marylou Tyler

APPENDIX D: SALES TOOLS AND SOFTWARE DIRECTORY

- Salesforce: CRM and Sales Automation
- HubSpot: Inbound Marketing and Sales Software
- LinkedIn Sales Navigator: Social Selling Tool

APPENDIX E: INDUSTRY ASSOCIATIONS AND NETWORKS

- Sales Enablement Society
- American Association of Inside Sales Professionals (AA-ISP)
- Technology Services Industry Association (TSIA)

APPENDIX F: FREQUENTLY ASKED QUESTIONS

Q: What is the best approach to lead generation in IT sales?
A: A combination of inbound and outbound strategies, leveraging content marketing, SEO, and personalized outreach.

Q: How can I improve my sales pitch?
A: Focus on understanding the customer's needs, crafting a compelling value proposition, and practicing your presentation skills.

APPENDIX G: INDEX

- Account-Based Marketing (ABM): 207
- AI and Machine Learning: 191, 305
- Customer Relationship Management (CRM): 55, 165
- Lead Generation: 92, 130
- Sales Enablement: 199, 225